AF430838

If, as Simone Weil once wrote, "absolutely unmixed attention is prayer," then the poems of Benjamin Cutler are prayers, blessings, devotions to the art of being here with others and ourselves. "I intend to hear everything," Cutler writes, and so he guides us into the "wild silence" to teach us, again and again, how to listen—to everything, to "every prayer that salts the air," to the "hopeless cries in the orange night," to the "marrow mystery" of our own miraculous being. The great "promise," he writes, "begins with wild silence." And so, with this *Wild Silence*, it does.
—Joseph Fasano, author of *The Crossing*


Where do wild silences live? Within our bodies, our memories, our griefs? Or are they an omnipresent force pulsing in the natural world beneath our feet? Perhaps they dwell in the violent code of survival and passion that all beings live by as *They know no song but their own / hunger.* In Benjamin Cutler's collection *Wild Silence* poem after poem illustrates how we all exist in the unsteady places between what is wild in our own natures, our planet, our families and earthly beauties that stun us into silence. How they embody all that we touch, love and see. How we remain *clawed yet gentle and unafraid of the dark.*
—Tina Schumann, Poetry Editor, Wandering Aengus Press and author of
  *Praising the Paradox*

# Wild Silence

Benjamin Cutler

trail to table press
eastsound, washington

First Edition. Published by Trail to Table Press
an imprint of Wandering Aengus Press

Poetry
ISBN: 979-8-218-33817-6
Author Photo: Clay Nations
Cover Image: Cosmic Kiss by Nancy Canyon
Book Design: Jill McCabe Johnson

Trail to Table Press
PO Box 334  Eastsound, WA 98245
trailtotable.net
wanderingaenguspress.com

For Jennifer,
whose love fills every silence.

# Contents

*I cannot be weaned*
*Off the earth's long contour, her river-veins.*

-Seamus Heaney

# An Invitation to Light

What is distance but a failure
of light?—light pulled

to its listless terminus, a rope
grown heavy with reaching. Take,

for instance, the third and fourth folds
of mountains: how they pale

like lips bruised blue with need
of breath; how, from my distant seat

behind this window, these peaks lose
laurels and pines, rivers and vines:

courageous greens that never feared
to be so gray.

And what of your window?—where
the light fails me entirely, where

you read these lines
despite this failing. Friend:

let us tie each frayed photon
into a new, far-reaching braid.

Light needs such quiet, gentle work.

# The Virtue of River Stone

The virtue of river stone
                     (That good stone—
the boulder in the creek where we swam
those fraying teen summers away:
Michael—not the angel, but an angel
still—rested there as on an altar, bare
and bright, arms spread at his sides
like resting wings, his water-
dazzled skin luminous against the story
of his ribs, as clean and pale
as secret devotions. We believed
we were the gods of every riverbank and dark current, and now—
in the retelling—we are.)
                         is in how it loses
itself to water's persistent and patient brush:
the hard and unforgiving edges of truth
weathering—smoothing—to myth.

# The Kissing Rock

My children point it out every time we pass—
as we hike the old and familiar creek-side
trail—and remind me of how I used to wade

through the shallows to climb upon that ancient
tabletop where I'd loll with the girls of my youth.
What my children know is merely the legend

of their imaginings: the strange beast
of their boyhood father, the mythic beauties
before their mother. In truth,

there was only one—as common and true
as a Carolina lily. I knew her name well
and the sound of my own when she'd call to me

over the rush of water and wind
from her place at the kissing rock's top.
I was as shy then as a riverbed shadow

and never knew her lips, only her creek-
wet hand in mine as we lay side-by-side, our sun-
warmed skin dappled by summer-leaf shade.

Our bright youth was so slight upon that cold,
immovable, gray weight of years—our quiet
promises carried away by the insistent

water passing below, forever flowing somewhere
beyond us: from river to river to ageless river.

# Prelude to Aubade

    In the dark summer air,
there is a voice that breaks

    a question into two desperate
notes. I intend to hear everything

    the cricket cries before sunup,
but my intentions

    have always been hidden
in the gasp between sleep

    and dawn. Still the cricket chimes:
*how / now—now / how*—and here I am,

    voiceless and wanting a song
I will never learn to sing before the red

    daylight demands its answers.

# Aubade: Omen



Two house sparrows, orbiting one another
from the left of morning, interrupt
my path—or I theirs—

as I drive through my workplace parking lot.
One bird arrows to the cover of a curbside oak
while the other, like a slung stone, strikes

steel and, caught in a cruel calculus, arcs
onto the center of my hood—solid, still,
and small—where it dies, where I watch it die

as I continue to my designated parking spot.
And though saddened—very probably
horrified—I am grateful to at least have an omen

on which to blame the day's
forthcoming collisions. What if I tell you
that before I even turn off the ignition

I am already thinking about this poem?
Let's not scavenge a metaphor. This quiet softness
is already the answer to every morning question.

# When

Tonight, the unyielding
sky is an anvil waiting
for heat and hammer,
and I wish I were

a blacksmith—hands
hardened with heavy,
practiced precision.
I might, then, forge

this night's question
into an answer. Tell me:
What is an answer
but a question balanced,

sharpened—ready
to split you open.

# The Lovers' Prayer to the Body

O musk & mineral,      salt-slick lips—each
                       pore's lifted hair a language only felt;

O marrow-mystery,      where bone softens to red
                       breath & healing's quiet machinery.

We worship skin &      bone but what of meat?
                       It is muscle's movement we resent:

push & pull & will.    Let us be still.
                       Let us be still. O let us be still.

# Thank You

*for Jennifer*

The windowless room
in which you love me
has no roof.
How else
would the light get in
—how else the rain?

*

The roofless room
in which I love you
has no floor.
How else
would the earth know
the curve of our bodies

*

drying together
under a new day's sun?

# The Dance



*We're the only real people here. The rest of them, they're only shadows.*
    —Frank Sinatra in *The Joker is Wild*

Swing your solid hips
        against the swaying darkness.

        Forget about the false
light and its soundless contrasts

until the music stops.
        And the music will stop.

        It is useless to count anything,
even whispered promises—a beat is a beat

is a beat—and every measured step
        is over as it begins.

        A hand is offered, a shoulder loaned,
a waist borrowed; nothing is kept

in the silence,
        and the silence always follows.

        It's simple: just move
with someone in your arms.

# Self-Portrait as Oyster
### (Galway, Ireland; Clarenbridge Oyster Bed)

I have no pearl, but you have
never wanted one—only to pucker

my pearlescent skin with lemon.
See how I quiver at this acid touch?

This is how you know I am
good, how you know I will

fill your mouth with cool ocean.
But do you know how

many have come before me, pulled
from this bed where river meets sea,

where fresh meets salt—
and for how many seasons of harvest?

Even Yeats, in his dark and ancient
tower, must have known us—Yeats

who loved a woman above his station
and then her daughter, too,

who was the image of her mother.
Perhaps they tasted my kind as well,

but I am not a meal for poets
or lovers, daughters or mothers. Taste me,

yes, but you will not be filled.
You will not remember me

by white stone or stony shell
but by the mineral-sweet surf

on your tongue—a brine
which will linger until washed away

and, like evening tide, another
rises to your lips.

O how like a gray moon I shine
and wane, sliding into your horizon.

# Their Father Is Sleeping or Walking

*The zone of silence. The zone of loneliness.*
*The zone of love. For me it is the only zone.*
                    —Anna Kamieńska

        Their father is sleeping or walking, and his hands
are numb. As he sleeps or walks

        into another warm night or day, the amber
queen fills another boxed comb with pearl-

        white brood in the humming dark,
her magnificent abdomen

        dipping dutifully into each deep cell
to kiss its floor; the black

        tadpoles erupt from their clear jelly and take
to skimming warm mud, insensible

        to the air above them into which they will leap,
in only weeks, with strange new legs; the silver cat

        with scabbed ears catches another fat and eyeless
mole, tears its gray throat, and abandons the soft,

        splayed body at the abandoned garden's edge;
two riverbank poplars at the father's childhood

        home—giants who have given their roots'
earth to countless stormed currents—drop

        into the river a week before the radiant flowering;
and the old magnolia stands, waits for the hungry

        black beetles to come to the pale and stainless
flesh of each broad petal to taste gold stamen.

        While their father sleeps or walks, he takes
a magnolia leaf from a low branch and holds it in a dream-

        numb palm. This dark leaf is a spear
point, a letter of parting, an apology, a love-

        bitten tongue, a broken feather
ready for mending—every green and vital question

he will not answer. He drops the leaf
or keeps it for his children—who are calling him

to wakefulness or home. He answers
five times and still speaks

nothing. He now knows, as blood burns
his waking hands, a long and living

promise begins with wild silence—

To My Eldest at the Age of Burning

> *Pigs experience hope, which we know because if raised in decent conditions*
> *they anticipate that pleasurable things will happen to them.*
> —Barbara J. King, NPR.org


Listen:
I once spoke with a man who worked
on a pig farm. This labor is not what he wanted,
but wanting meant nothing to him—only need.
*When the farm burned, you could smell*
*the smoked shit and flesh for miles,*
he said, *like someone mistook the smokehouse*
*for the outhouse.* His left hand was lame
and bandaged—not from blistering but a needle
meant for a pig's hip. His work had been to dose
and sort—syringe in one fist, ink in the other:
stab and stripe, stab and stripe, stab and stripe—
until needle broke against a thumb's thick knuckle.
*I wasn't working that shift,* he said, *so I didn't hear*
*their screams—but I imagine them.*
Listen:
Can you hear them, Son—all those hopeless
cries in the orange night? I remember
yours at the threshold of your bedroom door—
how the disorder became too much,
how a friend's farewell became too much,
how the Adderall became too much:
stab and stripe, stab and stripe, stab and stripe—
your tear-wet face against my chest.
I do not have to imagine your cries. We cleaned,
your mother and I, clearing and sorting the wreck
and waste—until, after the hours piled upon years,
and almost too late, I found your clutter-
buried heart, needful and ablaze, where
it nearly set fire to us all.

II

## Eve Knew—

       God would not always watch.
Even now, long after

       those first millennial lifespans, red
mounds of clay rise at the eastern edge

       of our widening garden of name-
marked stone—each shovelful displaced

       by another one of us gone cold
as new knowledge. She knew everything

       other than nakedness is a vain
myth of protection—and every fig

       leaf will wilt. Why wait until then?
A rib enters our sweat-cursed earth

       for every prayer that salts the air.
She knew you must dare to taste

       the forbidden—now, in your god-
crafted hand: ripe, redolent,

       sweeter than any commandment.

# Elegies of Gathering

**I**

When I first heard his father cry, I mistook
the lamentation for laughter. How could I—
a boy who had lost nothing, not even his way—
know anything of how
                          a heart can crack
against the belly, spill from the mouth, and thicken
the air? I should tell you
                          they sat in the kitchen
and how his mother took my hand—her work-
hardened thumbs against my un-callused knuckles—
and wet my wrist with her tear-softened cheek.
*Don't ever be so stupid, so stupid,*
                     *don't ever be,* she said,
and because I could not stand the sight of grief
mingled with promise, I looked away into the basket-
held silence of her fresh brown eggs—gathered by her
son the morning before we gathered to mourn him.

**II**

These counted years later, I—a man who has not lost
everything—can think only of the chickens, our three
hens lost in the dusk
                        of last summer's storm;
of how the drenched dark kept them from the roost's
dry refuge; of how they did not return in the dawn's
clean light, the light of a rainless day; and of how we baked
the last of their laying into a cake
                            as sweet as forgiveness
and ate it warm with our bare and blameless hands.

**III**

Did I tell you there were eggs in the kitchen where grief
filled the air like laughter? Did I tell you how grief
and laughter both begin in the belly?
                                        Watch with me, love:
I see a father and a mother the morning after
a night of rain. She takes three eggs—no, two—
in her practiced hands, cracks and whips them well
into a buttered pan. He fries, salts, and serves—
a shared meal from a shared plate.
                                Did I tell you, love—
yes, I must have—how a belly promises only to empty
and always knows what it needs?
                                Can you see them, love?
Yes, you must now. They cry (or laugh) as they share
what steams between them. He washes, she dries, they walk
outside—walk together to gather the new day's
eggs in the early morning fog,
                                enough light to see the love-
worn way through bowing grass, enough to reach into a nest
and feel what is round, warm, and not yet broken.

# Elegy: Fog and Forage

Night's final breath clouds the day,
hides what I already know: the dead,

fallen oak rooted to this side
of our stream that never dries,

now a branched and broken bridge
that crosses into the blue

forested valley where mushrooms
fruit—like revised memories—

from mycelium as old and alive
as a million griefs.

*

Here, we walked
and foraged. Here, we found

enough to fill ourselves
before the harsh day could dissolve

our shared ghosts and brief
mysteries. What we gathered,

you cleaned and I cooked—tasted
earth and butter on each other's lips.

*

Today, I search
only for the place where you left

enough for another day's harvest.
Let the inevitable light rest a little longer;

I want nothing
to do with fogless mornings.

# Elegy with Failed Metaphors

Near the end, Nana bit the end—
the tail—of a fish. This is not a metaphor.
I am tired of metaphors for dying;
it already swims in mystery-
dark waters. Nana, forgetting
her Southern-polished propriety, lifted
the fish from the plate and held it
between newly polished nails—stilled
in a moment of watery mis-remembrance—
then brought the gleaming gray
glory to her mouth. This was nothing
like a kiss and gentler than love's
                  young teeth; no, love's
                  barbed hook; no, love's
                  cast net. No, I am tired

of metaphors for loving. Nearer the end,
Nana bit nothing. The final stroke
left her submerged and swimming
in a sea for which we had no map,
no ship—her blue-scaled legs treading
memory's black brine, neck stretching
for air, until at last she found the moon-
                  glassed surface; no, the sun-
                  softened shore; no, the ocean's
                  skyless floor. No, I am tired

of metaphors, tired of these meatless
fins, tired of biting into nothing
but bone and skin. This is only
                  dying and loving.
                  We do them every day.

# The Gun, the Turntable

What Papa gave away
before his death: the knives—

Old Timers, Cases—antique folders
for every grandkid's pocket;

the leather-bound books he had
never read but wished he had;

the weed trimmer he had used
on his river-stone walkway

before the path had been replaced
with a pine-board ramp;

his father's revolver
he had only fired once; the turn-

table on which he had played
the smooth crooners of his youth.

*

What Papa wanted back
before his death, when all he knew
was that his hands were empty: everything.

*

What Papa asked for
before his death: the gun,
the turntable—and he raged

for their return, believed
the night's common scuffs
to be intruders at the door, wept

in bewildered grief
when his records could find
no needle to conjure a note.

*

What Papa demanded
before his death: not to cut, read, or clear,

but something solid
to aim at the night—and a song

to calm the silence: voices
like memories warbling in the dark.

# Dressing My Father-in-Law for Burial

I would have tied the tie differently:
full Windsor, centered and snug
against the white, pressed collar.

But his oldest son wanted the job—
and who could deny him this right?

So I watched—half Windsor,
knot too tight, loop overly loose
around the unbuttoned neck

as though the man were ready
for his after-work commute.

See him now, this grieving son—
hands atremble and earnest—tying
Dad's final tie: inexpertly, imperfectly.

But isn't this how any of us love?—
the only way we know how.

# Preemptive Lamentation for a Glacier

> I will sing for you,
before the coastline of my courage sinks
into this swollen surf, of how I waited
until a long day's dusk to pray for my father—
ignorant then that prayer is nothing
but steam rising from sunned ice. *We'll know
soon if it's hot,* Mom said of the rebellious
flesh invading his snowy chest—a poison
in lung and bone.
> I will sing for you
of how he will not go quietly or without voice—
as I've always imagined a silent giant would—
but in a language I am only now learning
to understand but cannot yet speak: water's
angry protest, the white wail of a river
surprised to be parting from its old
solid self, flooding into its own blood-
warm expanse.
> I will sing for you
that should he spread his absence over us
like a rising sea, it will be during a winter
morning that has forgotten winter—where
the once-frozen ground is muddied with fallen
prayer pouring from our palms, where the *scuff*
of a spade slicing into a false summer's
soil is the repeating sound of our grief.
Earth should not be so easily broken.

## While Wandering the Blue Ridge, We Followed the River Acheron


*I am haunted by waters.*
                    -Norman Maclean


**I**


We were young and lost and the water
was white—cloud-bright as it splayed
over the river's dark knuckles

and clear in the eddying pools
of its palms—and so we believed
the flow as fresh as a fawn's first breath.

We filled ourselves with river, wetting
our chins and necks with the recklessness
of the thirsty and unbroken. What we took

was ours, and from that tasting we hiked
upstream and listened to the water's
rush: the cold voices of our numberless

dead; though we could not understand
a single wet word, we learned—for the lost
—every river is the River Acheron.

**II**

Caught between the river's blunt teeth—
as skinless and broken as an answerless question—

the dead doe did not rest; there is no rest
where water floods ribs and pushes like a cry

through a jawless mouth. We looked and knew then
what we had tasted: every flavor is touched by loss.

Water, too, will take and remember what it has taken.
When you drink, know this: every mouth is a window

open to the rain. Is not each body a house haunted
by memory? Is not each memory a ghost of water?

**III**

The long way back: the tender, trembling

sky opened like a wound—each clear drop

returning to Earth like renewed memories

of our first gods. What could we do but keep

to the trail and praise the rain on our skin?

# I Know a Ghost

I know a ghost who arrives in the fall
to watch weary leaves pass
through her open palms—then vanishes
when the last tree is bare. I know

another who winters on the frozen
banks of a creek where he used to fish
and hides in the cold, wet grays
of iced stone and January flows. I know

a pair of ghosts who float together
into the branches of blossoming redbuds
just to feel something bloom
where their hearts once beat. I know

a ghost who knows only one song
and sings it to the tempo of a summer
storm: an infinite refrain arranged
in the key of a favorite memory,

composed with the notes of an unlived day.

# The Boy Who Hunts

out of season tells me
the fatty meat behind a deer's eye,
if eaten raw and right

after the kill, tastes
like dough—and he laughs
when he says it: *The doe*

*tastes like dough.* I believe
him—believe his tongue
knows the salty and shapeless

taste of uncooked bread,
and his young trigger-
callused fingers the slick

release of a dead eye
pried from a still-warm socket
that would have held it well

to see another waking
spring, through summer's green
abundance, into the treacherous fall.

*

This boy who hunts
out of season tells me he leaves

the body where it lies
to bloat like a yeasted loaf,

and I believe him—believe
he knows nothing

of the full and warm flavor
of patience; nothing

of any season save his own
hard and violent weather;

nothing of living,
gentle eyes

and the sweetness
that rises behind them.

# The Antlered Boy

*After Ansel Elkins*

The antlered boy is here
again at the lake's quiet edge.

This is the time for testing,
for rut, for clashing murderous
brow against murderous brow,

but he has left the other wild
boys to their play and wrath

        *

and has taken, yet again, the gray rope
into his scabbed hands—the ancient
rope that stretches from the water's black

surface, a surface that now trembles
with his every desperate heave.

        *

Each night he promises
his own warm heart

the new day will be different: the unyielding

rope will yield, the drowned
boat will rise from its lakebed sleep,

        *

and this antlered boy
will paddle to the farthest

shore where he will shed
his antlers, leave them

to the lake's currents, walk
into the foreign forest, and build

his own small fire

        *

with which he will warm his hands
and cast a crownless shadow—
blue and rippling into the strange night.

*

For now, a whippoorwill
cries across the water—invisible,

insistent, questioning the dark.
Our antlered boy hears

but still—unmoved—pulls
the rope. This is the lonesome

work of every exile,
and it is not yet time for rest.

# Snake and Deer

The solitary snake crosses the creek.
He is as blue and quiet as a morning
ripple as he ribbons through each silver

wave—and though his body is as lithe
as water, this dark swimmer holds his venom-
free head high and wants only the solid

bank on the other side where the smooth
granite is as warm as a long summer
secret and the bowing grass will keep him

    as safe as shadow. Here the lone deer sees

his slick silence, watches him slip into hidden
passage, and dips her soft and ready tongue
into the pool she knows so well, tastes

every mineral the water carries—the earthy
alchemy of animal, plant, and rock. She rises
and steps into the speckled day, her broad ears

full of blooded light. Here these rovers are gods
who know nothing of worship, only the demands
of hunger and thirst, red sun and shade—the old

    steady seasons of crossing and returning.

Ophiolatry

The skins brought the boy back again
        and again to the abandoned single-wide
in the woods—empty as a forgotten temple

        stripped of its rites. Diamond
patterns, copper parchments, the dead sheet
        music of a rattler's shell: old promises

on windowsills—abandoned offerings
        on dusty shrines. He moved from worship
to worship, touching, with his naked hands,

        the scales of each hollow ghost: reverent
modes of discipleship he knew well. Hidden
        husks of the living, the risk and blood-

rush of hope and fear: the possibility
        of a venomous strike. His pious parents
knew nothing of these new devotions

        and would have forbidden them
had they known—so he kept his prayers
        as secret as any shedding faith,

as silent as the slow and sacred violence
        of a soul sloughing its own worn image.

# The Black Snake on My Lawn

Ancient instinct warned
it should die, but I thought better of it—
of how I should not crush its head

when it had never bruised my heel,
never hissed in my ear; of how
its only cruelty had been to swallow

a cricket's bright song into its own black,
satin-scaled silence. So, fallen branch
in hand, I urged this slender living

shadow to my land's eastern edge—
where the earth is richer than dust or days,
where dark ivy creeps up every tree

and covers a multitude of sins.

# Devil's Walking Stick

> All souls that sting and gather
> against hunger congregate here, and they make
> a chorus of their harvest—because what else is there
>
> in the midday heat but this gold
> flowering at the crest, this last and solitary blessing
> of the year's longest days? Such a late communion—
>
> a high and brimming bounty,
> a nectar-rich crown the flightless cannot reach
> unwounded. Come, fallen wanderer, take this tree
>
> in your grip; cut it from glory
> to walk upon this earth. Why look to Heaven
> when the path is root-mapped, underfoot and deeper
>
> still? Every Son of the Morning
> knows blooming is brief, knows the hike into evening
> is long and requires a thorn-bloodied palm. Arrive
>
> and listen, stained staff in hand:
> the night is also full of song—each voice a solo
> in the cool and flowerless dark, waiting in the dew
>
> for your shadow-sung answer.

Should you depart in the morning,

your boots' crunch
along your blood-

kin's secret trail
will send the cottontails

bounding into the brambles.
Mind their fear only a little,

only enough to remember
you mean no harm

until you enter the dawn-
fogged creek. A warning:

root and rock will break
your ankle with no thought

toward justice—or mercy.
Wade carefully. Present

gently. Remember: you are
not here. Keep the line

slack, keep the line
tight, wait for the brook

trout to rise like water's
lightning to your offering.

Lift. Hold. Pull. Grip
lightly with wet hands

until the harm is done—
*so little harm,*

you will tell yourself,
*such bright beauty,*

you will tell yourself—
and release. Return home

by nightfall. Notice,
as you walk the darkened

path, the bat circling, sightless,
diving for waking moths;

notice the grace—notice
this swift and fearless art.

# Advice on Nighttime Caregiving

Know the bulk of night
will be sleepless and embrace it
with the weariest part of yourself.

Nothing but bitter tea will do,
steeped too long as you pour
another glass of water

another mouth will drink,
as you console another crying
child who values sleep

on different terms,
as you—deep in the black
hour when familiar constellations

wend into a strange topography—
walk the dog who will thank you
without language: she who eats

white clover by night,
sniffling through dark
grass sweetened with dew.

Now sleep or wake—let go
of what you hold. The untouched
tea is as cool as morning.

# It Is Summer and the Neighbors Are Yelling

I have stepped outside to listen.
The couple above—one lover
from one country, the other another—
yell because they are here,

together, trying to live the same story.
The couple below yell because
one lover is drunk and the other doesn't
drink enough. None of them know

how their voices, like neighborhood
sirens, have invited me to investigate—
a bystander at their wreckage, a quiet
voyeur with nothing to say.

*

In my own yard between us all, the hives
hum—two cedar boxes boiling with wild
colonies lured by the scent of their own past.

Their thrum is insistent, but the bees say
everything that matters with scent and dance:
the slow yellow arc of sun, a gray specter

of cloud, the flavors of fields and forests
beyond our road. Nothing concerns
these bees so much as the weather.

*

To the neighbors, still yelling: I will offer
this harvest of honey; a tongue can be silenced

with a drop of something sweet. Then, together,
we will listen: our breaths, our bees, our blue

horizon of nothing but so many whispers.
We wouldn't make out a single word.

# Seed of Summer's End

The mourning dove, who knows
much of mourning, hides

in the blossom-bare sour-
woods at the field's shadowed edge.

The ridge-peaked horizon,
which she has never measured,

is as blue and hazy as a childhood
memory. She weeps

her song, flies to the grass beneath
the empty feeder, and takes

what remains of seed, of morning,
of summer's wilting warmth.

# Autumn Note

When the year is old and you are left
to own its disappointments, take yourself—
as you must have done many times

when a leaf was nothing more than leaf,
before each tree's green spirit began
to retreat into its own wooden heart to sleep

deep through cold, before you understood
that to touch a thing is to be remembered by it—
up to the deep creek and leaf-covered trail

you've known all your life. Lie down
upon the cradle-rock you wish were a secret.
Let its sure weight brace you; let it

pull from you the heat you have held
so desperately—so obediently—until
you know that you too are earth.

Look into the yellowing canopy—notice
how each released leaf whorls earthward
in a final dance entirely its own. Consider:

the pace of a tree, the aged silence of rock,
how the perfect language of water-
sound never forms a single question.

# Early Snow

This first snow does not belong
to winter but to fall. Flakes, clotting

in the clouds like last night's vespers,
return to us—bloated and abundant—

and cover nothing. Each soul-
thin sliver, magnified under our eyes,

would seem to us so masterfully
measured and carved—cold and silver

stars wrought by the good air's fingers.
We might marvel at such excess,

but see how these glassy frailties hold
to one another? Desperate and sure

lovers. Still, they warm nothing.
Look: they fall as if to arrive

to their glory. The tired grass—as yellow
as a long year—welcomes their wet

vanishing as it would a common rain.
Too late. Too late to green again.

Too soon. Too soon to bear the white
and brilliant weight of all that promise.

# On the Year's First Morning

The rain has stained the pasture gray,
and still they have come—these two

small deer the very color of our sun-
less sky. They are apart, each near

the wooded edge, and together—
alone without a thought

of their shared solitude. With quiet care,
this unsheltered pair lower

their heads—the new January's water
spilling from their brows to the failing

grass where they graze what's left
of yesterday's year.

                  I would go to them—
leave my dry safety behind this window

and kiss, with my simple mouth,
the wet velvet of each ear and whisper

every warm blessing I know,
though my gods are few—if only

these careful deer would allow
such tame intimacy. I look away,

look again, and they are gone, hidden
in the dark pines who know nothing—

everything—of a year's turning.
*I would follow them*, I say. If only. If only.

# Here, Where I Sleep

The dogwood.
The redbud.

Neither will bloom
until I wake.

Between them:
the same silver

stream I hear
only when I read

wonder or write
grief or pray

to any forgotten god.
The high rushing

song of a thousand
timorous birds who flee

these low gray clouds.
Always, the season: white

winter: blue notes,
the voice

of falling snow
covering me

wholly—here,
where I sleep.

Then: morning, new
sun—my waking

body arched and wet.
Blossoms everywhere.

IV

# The Church of Unmaking



> *As a Christian, I believe that there is a creator in God who is much bigger*
> *than us. And I'm confident that, if there's a real problem, He can take care*
> *of it.*
>
> —Rep. Tim Walberg (R-Mich.) on climate change

Praise this absence. Praise
        the sky's birdless blue—the dead

blue of Spix's macaw, the cryptic
        treehunter's silenced cry,

the passenger pigeon's passing: sing
        a psalm for the final birdsong.

Praise the rhinos' hornless bones, stones
        among stone—western black

and northern white. Praise
        the must of hollow shells cleansed

of strange flesh: Pinta Island tortoise,
        Hawaiian tree snail. Let us crawl

into this emptiness we have made
        and name it the Church of Unmaking—

where we will worship what was
        and call it martyr,

where we will lick the walls to taste
        what was body and what was

blood, where we can hear
        the echo of our own voices

and call it God: *Take. Eat.*
        *This do in remembrance of me.*

# When We Believed the World Wouldn't End

After the final harvest, the forecast
called for freezing temperatures
and the end of this winsome world.

We have never trusted doomsday
news, but this new winter had been born
a living, wet, and hungry thing. We could feel

its ice-watered tongues pushing through
the walls, searching for our mouths. *Stand
here*, I said, *stand here and look.* The silvered

sun still knew itself and breathed its yellow
name through the window glass. *Wait. Listen,*
I said. *Doesn't it sound like our last warm day*

*of picking?* Yes: the apple orchard in fall,
the master's cider-drunken sleep, our love-
making behind the hives. You loved

the colony's scent: wax-ripened bread and apple-
blossom gold. The bees' thrum made you horny,
you said, because it was a music more ancient

than love. Our bodies became themselves then—
all petal-bloom and honey-gleam—each spill
and blood-warm bud a blessing of skin and sun

on our lips. The memory sung, we stepped
from the window's dying glow into the stone-
blue shadow—the dark of a winter-dead hive,

the dark of an ice-shattered tree. The tired sun
grew hoarse and the frosted tongues licked
their teeth. When I reached for your hand, I found

a blackened apple frozen to its branch. *The forecast
was right after all,* I tried to say, but my mouth
was brittle with cold, the words ice in my throat.

# A Prayer to the Technician Who will Upload Us to the Cloud

When you deliver us up to this modern
death—this latest model of immortality—
do so with ungloved hands. Leave fingerprints

on our untethered minds so each moved memory
will be more than a web of silicone and code,
more than a pixelated specter haunting a cloud,

more than merely a reminiscence of skin.

With the callused edges of your thumbs, close
our abandoned eyes—shuttered, rendered obsolete.
But let us keep a recollection of sight—let us save

our vocabulary of vision: an outmoded language
to signify how light bends, breaks, and mends
against a field of sweetgrass in wind—how green

shadows live and die with every shimmer.

Let our formless mouths not be synthetic,
silent, clean. Let us speak. Let us sing: salty,
purple, fibrous, and feral—voices redolent

of what is lost and altogether ancestral
so those who still have ears to hear will know
something came before this brave bloodless

forever—something earthborn came before.

# Ars Poetica at the End of the World

In the end there was a word
for everything, a single word

for everything, but in the end
it did not save us—

we who would only speak
in the language of an answer-

with-no-question. When our voices
finally failed us, we tried writing

the word over & over again,
like guilty children, tearing pages

from our books to wear
against the ash. We remembered

how the fishmongers of Denmark
& the carpenters of England

had worn yesterday's news
as hats—shielded from burn & stain

by want ads & weddings & births,
by predictions & crimes & deaths—

but our marks were lost
in the smoke's smear & our paper

with the embers. Had we known
this was the end,

we would have invented new words
to name our sorrows, new questions

to name our loves,
but we always believed

we were at the beginning
of something new. In the end

there was nothing to name
& nothing to name this nothing,

& in that void was the word—
with only the darkness to comprehend it.

# A Prophecy for the First Horse that Carried Me

*And I saw, and behold a white horse...*
<br>-Book of Revelation 6:2

Conquest followed by red
and black and pale—beasts
of conflict, judgement, and death.
But what of this equine quartet—

why should they care
for the end of days? I ask
because I know nothing
of horses, having ridden only one:

you, a worn mare with a coat
of parched earth. There is a photo,
and even I who know nothing
can see I knew nothing—

something about my bend
of legs and timid posture,
my hands shy and passive
on the reins. I remember

how you would trot and threaten
a canter, how I knew I could not
handle the gallop, how I knew you
could cast me from your back

to break me under hoof or against
some senseless pasture stone.
One can know much when he knows
nothing; there are portents

aplenty. Do you believe
these doomsday steeds will come
at last, and do you wish for their arrival?
Will you join them and find a new cause

to run? If the fire must follow
in your thunder and cloud,
let your herd of flame circle back
to these trampled fields

when my final season has passed—
spines unburdened, necks upon one
another's crests. And when you, long-
suffering and weary angel, bow

your heaven-heavy head to the earth, graze
the green that rises from such burning.

# Naming: The End of Mystery


*Do you pray?*
                    -A Friend


    Is this not prayer?—this longing
and praise, this naming

    and in the naming, finding
what should not be named.

    What was moon before *moon,*
*rock, dust,* before the orbiting

    astronaut named this silver
mother of tides a *dirty*

    *beach?* Even the oceans rise
and foam with voiceless prayer

    to her pull. How much of this
landless frontier is unnamed?—depths

    too dark or aglow for naming.
Pray. Pray to that darkness,

    to that deep—pray—pray—
and do not make the mystery

    common with naming.

# Petition



-Nick Cave, "Into My Arms"

If there is to be a heart, cavern the heart: tunnel
the rhythmed red muscle into a deep and unmapped cave
where something wild might wander, find shelter—clawed
yet gentle and unafraid of the dark. If there is to be dark,

body the dark—limb the darkness: tireless
legs that this shade might follow or carry the day-
weary traveler into rest, broad hands that it might cover
an anguished mouth. If there is to be a mouth,

flower the mouth: petal the lips and every tooth
and make of the tongue a bright stamen that it might call
to the winged gatherers who search the day for sweetness—
call with vibrant, soundless music. If there is to be music,

let it not be hymn, psalm, or lament—but music, music,
and only music. Let it sing. Let it deepen. Let it beat.

# Wading, I Hear Their Prayer

It is evening, and the elk
are calling their autumn

prayer from the wooded side
of the river in which I stand.

I am no god and never will be,
and so I can give no answer

but to myself: I hear you, dear
ones, in this darkening hour.

*

Though I cannot see the sun
beyond the canopy's cover,

I know it has not set. Not yet—
not until the bull's antlers bow

amen and the mother dreams
with her summer-raised calf.

The wild prayer continues.
The old river whispers.

# Three Wild Vespers

**I**

O lost, O wisp, O ghost-
pale moth—fearful

and flitting against the luminous
ceiling: my hands also glow

with borrowed light. Descend.
Be still. Stay with me. I will

carry you through the locked door
into summer's open night.

**II**

Rabbit in your burrow, quivering
like a fist: tomorrow's gold day is free

of tooth and claw, and the yellowed
fields are safe for your play

and your love. These gentled
fingers have left sweet autumn

roots in their dark soil—take and eat
as from a friend's harmless hand.

**III**

Ice-knuckled creek: remember
your summer bed and edge—

how each green rain or dry day
can swell or dwindle your flow.

Receive and hold my wintered palms
until ripe clouds gather for spring.

These cold hands also want a warm
storm to soften their cracked banks.

# A Final Geese Poem

What more can we say
about the geese? They know
better than to swim into the flood-

current—these fallen angels
who, for this gray moment,
have forsaken their courage.

See them now? Calm and treading
the far and vanishing bank, daring
themselves not to cross. Perhaps

such easy caution is enough
wisdom to survive a storm
this far from heaven.

# Birdsong in the Time of Quarantine

      I am living
on birdsong—

      the sunrise
reveries of the fog-

      silvered morning,
a busy hour

      I've never been still
enough to know

      until now, here.
I now know

      these bright,
varied melodies

      are not music
but the innate,

      lonesome cries
of the world's oldest

      need: hear me,
hear me, find me.

      But isn't this what
every song ever was?

      I—as quiet
as a broken syrinx—

      will never tire
of this: this

      din of desire,
this wild chorus

      of the new day's
ritual, this riotous

      waking into song.

# Ode: February Morning at Our Rural Café

The red-eyed nurse with his mask down
for now—only now—for the first and best
of the day's many cups. The young

grandmother who receives
the window's polished rays
against her face but does not squint

as she watches her small grandson—
who wears Halloween pajamas in this cold
month of love—trace tabletop flowers

with his soft finger. The retired artisan—in faded
barn coat—who talks of gathering deadfall locust
for the bassinet he will build but will not sell.

The ancient basset hound asleep
at the feet of a local pastor who speaks
of the poignant joys of final days—of taking

his wheelchair-bound and dying sister
to a pottery shop where they found the perfect
vase for her ashes: *How we laughed*

*and laughed,* he says, *when we left*
*and realized we had no lid.*
The grandson again, holding

his grandmother's hand as they step
through the bell-chiming door into the vague
light of day—unseasonable

mummies dancing on his back, so joyfully
suspended in their unraveling.

# Spring Break

Two teenagers—boys spring-breaking,
bare to the waist—pass their football
across the hotel pool, testing their precision
against the sea-salted breeze,
                              their laughter
a sunset-song only the young can sing.

Then it happens: the ball—thrown wide
and missed—rebounds against concrete
and careens into the pool where it is caught
like a fallen shard of night by angels
of blue-gold light.
                    The boys argue—the bright
banter of friends who have never fought
without a smile—over who goes in
until one relents, wades in up to his belly,
stiffens against the splash, and retrieves it.

They continue their stakes-free game,
neither believing they'll ever lose
a thing. And why would they?
                            Here—so far
from cold, from home, from whatever
they'll miss a week from now.

# Self-Portrait as Gardener, Garden, and Nighttime Rain

By morning, the rain is as silent as the sun-
    rise—no longer rain but what remains—
as though it hadn't harangued the garden
    through the whole of its first starless night. Innocent

tomatoes and blameless basil: each so achingly tender
    as to render hope both needful and perilous.
Here is the gardener at the garden's edge. He stands
    where he knelt the day before and placed the seedlings in new

earth, earth so lovingly laid and enriched for young
    roots, roots now baptized beyond saving—or just to the edge
of redemption. But this is nothing. What gardener
    has ever had a say about the sky? Loss is no surprise.

What amazes is how this wet day dazzles in the clear
    morning—defiantly glitters in each branch, needle, and leaf,
soon to lift from its brilliance like a final breath: weightless,
    new and entirely itself. Watch this gardener

watch the light and forget the night's flood
    of questions. There is sun. There is earth. There is time.
O there is time—enough to plant what might wilt away
    or grow to ripe sweetness. Yes—there is enough time for that.

# The Fire

The fire you have built—here in what you believed
to be the lifeless, lonely dark—glows, cryptic
and alive, into the moonless night.

See how these wavering, watery shadows dance
with every rock, root, trunk, leaf, and flitting moth.
See how these phantoms of fire take

the forms of your nightmares, dreams, memories,
and loves (lost and found), some the very likeness
of your hidden hopes. Come closer, friend,

to these flames; feel the warmth you have made.
Do not let it die. When you leave, keep
a glowing coal to carry with you wherever you go.

# The River at World's End

                  does not flow over the edge
but from it—the headwaters beyond the first silver
shimmers of star-shine, where the lake of our oldest
light laps at the shores of every mystery, and wave-
song is the pulse of our blood's oldest hymn: a voiceless
lay we have always known, since before love ever needed
language to sustain it.
                 That wordless psalm never begs,
but sings a question composed only for you—a call-
and-response as ancient as water, each note a tributary
swelling the chorus—and you will
                       answer: become a new-
scaled creature and swim upstream. No river, not even this first
and last river, promises arrival—only passage, both patient
and perilous. Beware

*

              the watchful osprey perched riverside
and high on a leafless branch; the lean, pale heron wading
and wandering in the riffles; the dark, quick-pawed otter flirting
with the river's shadows. They know no song but their own
hunger—an endless refrain in which you are nothing
but a single red note. Beware
                  the barefoot boys who fish
from the banks and shin-deep eddies. Their faces are yours,
and with the practiced patterns of your life's measured seconds,
they cast bright flies tied
              in the image of every fond memory
(and every shame, too)—dry parachutes that never sink but dance
darkly on the gold-rippled surface.

*

                But should you rise
from your safe channel or secret pool—should you bite—
these gentle boys, after the rod-bending bout, will pull
the perfect hook from your gasping mouth and return you,
lip-bloodied and spent, to your sun-veined stream.
Your panicked heart will slow—
               return—to the timeless
meter of that old verse that echoes from every watershed.
With the rhythm of each fin's flex keeping steady time,
swim on. Follow that call.
            You can hear it beating even now.

# Last Lap Around the Dead

During my last
lap at the cemetery

I wish
to join the dead

in their cool-earth
rest—muscle's slow

fall from bone, forgetting
its flex and pull

and rhythms, skin
giving up sweat-

shine for the dry
dark. But when

the run is done,
that old sun

a morning-young star,
I lie above these silent

sleepers—my back to their arm-
crossed breasts—and remember:

O breath—O grass—O wind-
whispering oak—

O light—O light—O half
the day is light.

# ACKNOWLEDGEMENTS

Gratitude to the editors of the following publications in which these poems first appeared, some in a slightly different form.

*Appalachian Review*: "Devil's Walking Stick" and "Elegies of Gathering"

*Barren Magazine*: "To My Eldest at the Age of Burning"

*Blue Mountain Review*: "Ars Poetica at the End of the World" and "Last Lap Around the Dead"

*CaldwellArts.com*: "The River at World's End"

*Cumberland River Review*: "The Black Snake on My Lawn"

*Diode Poetry Journal*: "Their Father is Sleeping or Walking" as "The Father is Sleeping or Walking"

*Diologist*: "Dressing My Father-in-Law for Burial"

*EcoTheo Review*: "Early Snow"

*North Carolina Literary Review*: "Ode: February Morning at Our Rural Café"

*O'Henry*: "Advice on Nighttime Caregiving" (also in *PineStraw Magazine* and *Walter*)

*Orange Blossom Review*: "While Wandering the Blue Ridge, We Followed the River Acheron"

*Pinesong: Awards Anthology of the North Carolina Poetry Society*: "Self Portrait as Oyster" as "Self-Portrait as an Oyster from the Clarenbridge Oyster Bed in Galway," "The Church of Unmaking," "Petition," and "A Prayer to the Technician Who Will Upload Us to the Cloud"

*Psaltery & Lyre*: "A Prophecy for the First Horse that Carried Me"

*River Heron Review*: "Elegy with Failed Metaphors"

*Tar River Poetry*: "On the Year's First Morning"

*The Broadkill Review*: "Should you depart in the morning," and "The Boy Who Hunts"

*The Dodge*: "Three Wild Vespers" as "Three Wild Vespers: Hands"

*The Lascaux Review*: "When We Believed the World Wouldn't End"

*The Shore*: "An Invitation to Light"

*The West Review*: "Elegy: Fog and Forage" and "Here, Where I Sleep"

*Under a Warm Green Linden*: "Birdsong in the Time of Quarantine"

*Willows Wept Review*: "Autumn Note" and "Self-Portrait as Gardner, Garden, and Nighttime Rain"

*Zone 3*: "Preemptive Lamentation for a Glacier" as "Preemptive Elegy to a Glacier in this Time of Melting," and "The Virtue of River Stone"

"The Lovers' Prayer to the Body" first appeared in the novel *Even as We Breathe* by Annette Saunooke Clapsaddle (University Press of Kentucky, Fireside Industries, 2020)

"I Know a Ghost" and "The Fire" first appeared in Calliope Stage Company's 2022 stage production "Calliope Shorts: Campfire Stories."

Additional and endless gratitude to the many who supported my journey through these poems: editors and judges who honored my work through awards and nominations; the judges and board of the Susan Laughter Meyers Fellowship for their gift of time through the Weymouth Center Residency during which much of this collection took its shape; Dawn Gilchrist for her insight, encouragement, and always-gentle honesty; the editors of Wandering Aengus Press for believing in my work and releasing it into the world, especially Editor in Chief, Jill McCabe Johnson, and Poetry Editor Tina Schumann for her incredible manuscript critiques; Esteban Rodríguez, Jessica Jacobs, and Joseph Fasano for their generous words of endorsement; and to my dear wife, partner, and best friend, Jennifer Cutler, whose love and support have been and are more expansive and sure than any poem.

# About the Author

Benjamin Cutler is an award-winning poet and author of the full-length books of poetry, *The Geese Who Might be Gods* (Main Street Rag, 2019) and *Wild Silence* (Trail to Table Press, 2024). His poetry has been nominated for the Pushcart Prize numerous times and has appeared in *Zone 3*, *Verse Daily*, *Tar River Poetry*, and *EcoTheo Review*, among many others. He is also a recipient of the North Carolina Poetry Society's Susan Laughter Meyers Poetry Fellowship. In addition, Benjamin is a high-school English and creative writing teacher in the Southern Appalachian Mountains of western North Carolina where he lives with his family and frequents the local rivers and trails.

BenjaminCutlerPoet.com

9 798218 338176